Bull Rider

Marilyn Halvorson

orca soundings

ORCA BOOK PUBLISHERS

Library and Archives Canada Cataloguing in Publication

Halvorson, Marilyn, 1948–
Bull rider / Marilyn Halvorson.

(Orca soundings)
ISBN 10: 1-55143-233-1 / ISBN 13: 978-1-55143-233-5

1. Rodeos--Juvenile fiction. I. Title. II. Series.

PS8565.A462B84 2003   jC813'.54   C2002-911488-8
PZ7.H168Bu 2003

First published in the United States, 2003
Library of Congress Control Number: 2002116519

Summary: Layne is determined to be a bull rider
like his father—who was killed by a bull.

Orca Book Publishers gratefully acknowledges the support for its
publishing programs provided by the following agencies: the Government
of Canada through the Canada Book Fund and the Canada Council for the
Arts, and the Province of British Columbia through the BC Arts Council
and the Book Publishing Tax Credit.

Cover photography by Eyewire

Orca Book Publishers
PO Box 5626, Stn. B
Victoria, BC Canada
V8R 6S4

Orca Book Publishers
PO Box 468
Custer, WA USA
98240-0468

www.orcabook.com
Printed and bound in Canada.
Printed on 100% PCW recycled paper.
13 12 11 10 • 9 8 7 6

To Wes and Chad, whose real-life experience made the book work.

Chapter One

I was sitting at the kitchen table writing when Mom came in. "Hi, Layne," she said, setting down a bag of groceries. "Doing your homework already?" she asked with a grin. "You sure you're feeling all right?"

Any other time I would have grinned back. Mom has to nag me so much about homework that it's a joke between us.

But this time I didn't crack a smile. I was too nervous. "It's not homework," I said slowly, looking up at her.

She shrugged and crammed some lettuce in the fridge. "No?" she said, only half listening. "What is it then?"

I swallowed. "An entry form for the rodeo next month," I said and watched her grin fade. I knew it would be like this. It had been like this the other two times I had tried. But it wouldn't be quite the same this time. Because this time I wasn't backing down.

Mom slowly closed the fridge and came over to the table. She never took her eyes off me until she picked up the paper. Then she glanced at it, crumpled it up and threw it on the table. "No, Layne," she said in a tight voice. Her eyes met mine again. "Not the bull riding. You know how I feel about that."

I knew all right. We'd been through this scene so many times it was like living in an instant replay. But this time I fought back. "Yeah, and you know how I feel about it too."

"I don't care how you feel," Mom shot back. "All I know is that I watched a bull kill my husband and there's no way I'll risk watching one kill my son."

I stood up fast—and almost knocked the table over. "Oh, come on, Mom, it won't happen."

"You bet it won't happen," Mom cut in before I could finish. "The answer is no," she said, grabbing her jacket and heading for the door. That's the way she always tried to end things. Get in the last word and then get out of there. But I wasn't going to let her do it this time.

"You can't stop me," I said in a flat voice. That got her attention. She spun around. Mom and I have more in common than our blue eyes and blond hair. Our tempers match too. Her eyes flashed angrily, but before she could say anything I cut her off. "Give me a break, Mom," I said. "I'm almost seventeen."

Mom laughed—but she didn't sound happy. "Right, Layne, almost. Just another eight months till your birthday." Then, in a voice hard as steel, she added, "And I've got news for you. As long as you're living in this house, I can stop you. And don't you ever forget it."

I looked her straight in the eye. "If that's the way it's gotta be," I said slowly, "I can always get out of this house. But I'm gonna ride."

Right then I realized what I'd done. Backed myself into a corner. You didn't push my mom like that and get away with it. What if she called my bluff? Leaving home was the last thing I wanted to do. Living on the ranch meant hard work, long hours and a lot of responsibility, but it was the only life I knew. And I didn't want to lose it.

Mom and I stood there for a minute, glaring at each other. Maybe she knew she was cornered too. Was she really tough enough to kick me out if I entered the bull riding?

Suddenly she glanced at her watch, gave a gasp and ran for the door. I was glad there wasn't time to finish this fight right now.

Mom's a nurse and works the late shift at the hospital in Greentree. It's hard to hold a steady job and keep the ranch going too, but she doesn't have much choice. The ranch isn't a great moneymaker—especially when you've got a family to support.

I heard her start the Jeep and burn out of the driveway. If I spun that much gravel, I'd hear about it.

I picked up the entry form and smoothed it out. It was in rough shape, but it would do the job.

"Cool move, Hot Shot." A voice behind me made me jump. It was Terror, of course, my kid sister. Her real name's Tara, but if you knew her you'd understand the nickname. I hadn't even known she was in the house, but I could bet she hadn't missed a second of that scene between Mom and me.

"What's that supposed to mean?" I snarled back at her.

"Don't you think Mom's got enough problems just keeping this place going? She sure doesn't need you getting her all upset."

Great. All I needed was a free guilt trip. Especially coming from the kid who was a disaster looking for a place to happen. Her adventures had landed her in the emergency room twice already this year. "Get off my case, Terr," I snapped. I pushed past her and headed for my room.

I changed into an old shirt. What I had in mind was real hard on clothes. As I turned to go out, the newspaper clipping on the wall caught my eye. It had been there so long it was yellow, but the headline still stood out: *One Ride Away from a Championship*.

The picture was clear too. My dad grinning from ear to ear right after he scored an 87 on his second last ride at the National Finals. It was the second last ride of his life too. On his next bull he hung up, got his hand caught in the rigging. The clowns were good. They got in there and distracted the bull and finally managed to jerk the rope loose. But it was too late. He was trampled so bad he never woke up.

That was six years ago, but it still seems like yesterday. I was ten years old and my whole world fell apart. With Dad gone there was a big hollow space inside of me that I thought nothing would ever fill. I used to lie awake at night thinking about him. About how bad he'd wanted that championship and how close he'd come to getting it.

Slowly, an idea had begun to take shape. Dad could never win that championship, but he could have the next best thing. His son could do it for him.

I've been working on it ever since. But it hasn't been easy. Oh, I've done a lot of steer riding. I was already entering the boys' steer riding before Dad died, and I kept at it. Mom didn't mind that. Steer riding isn't all that dangerous. Steers buck pretty good, and once in a while they might accidentally kick you after they unload you. But they're nowhere near as big as the bulls and they mostly just want to get away from you. A lot of Brahma bulls would really like to kill you after they dump you.

I'm too old to enter the steer riding now, so if I want to learn about riding bulls there's only one way to do it. By riding bulls. And that's where Jana Kelvin comes into the picture. We've known each other since grade one and she's always been a good friend. The last year or two I've been taking more note of the fact that she's also a girl. I think I'm going to do a little more work on combining those two words pretty soon. But, right now, what mattered most was the fact that Jana's dad raises rodeo stock. He also has a big indoor arena set up to try them out.

I stuffed my shirttail into my jeans and headed outside. I didn't make it. Halfway through the kitchen, Terror caught up to me. "You goin' down to Kelvins' arena again, Layne?"

I turned around. "What's it to you?" I said angrily. She wasn't supposed to know I was going there.

"Lots," she said. "'Cause if you are you can hook the trailer on and take Rambo and me with you. I want to practice barrel racing him in the arena."

Terror and Rambo. The perfect pair. Rambo was her horse and the name really fit. All great body and not enough brains to come in out of the rain. He might have the speed for a great barrel racing horse, but I didn't think he'd ever make it. He was too pig-headed. He'd just as soon run right over the barrels as do the figure-eight pattern around them.

Anyhow, there was no way I was about to haul that outlaw horse anywhere. Last time he was in the trailer he almost kicked a hole through it. Besides, I didn't want Terror along any more than I wanted her horse.

"Why should I take you?" I said. "What have you ever done for me?" I wasn't being completely fair.

Even though she had the temper of a pit bull on steroids, Terror wasn't such a bad kid sister. She'd covered for me more than once when I'd pulled some stunt I didn't want Mom to find out about. And, although I'd never admit it, I couldn't help but be kind of proud of Terror. She was totally fearless around animals and could handle any horse she ever climbed onto. I had a sneaking suspicion that if she'd been a boy she'd have beat me to a bull riding title.

But right now I wasn't in any mood to be fair. After that run-in with Mom I didn't feel like being anything but miserable.

Terror's eyes narrowed. "I've done plenty of things for you. But what you'd better worry about is what I'm gonna do to you if you don't take me along."

"Oh, wow," I sneered. "You're scarin' me to death."

She shrugged. "Okay, if that's the way you want it." She started to walk away.

I let her walk a dozen steps before I broke down. Assuming Terror was bluffing could be dangerous. "Well," I yelled after her, "what are you gonna do?"

She tossed her head. "Tell Mom that Jana Kelvin's been letting you use her dad's bulls to practice on."

We went out and loaded Rambo.

Chapter Two

We pulled up beside Kelvins' arena. Jana was waiting for us. I leaned out of the window of the truck. "Hi, Jana."

"Hi, Layne," she said with that great smile of hers. "Come to try to break your neck again?"

I grinned. "Sure, why not? Your parents still aren't home?" I asked cautiously. Jack Kelvin, Jana's dad, provides the broncs and bulls used in rodeos. He always has a few bulls that aren't ready to take to the rodeos yet. This was the fourth time I'd been down here riding some of them. Jana always made sure her parents weren't going to be around when I did it. Mom and the Kelvins were good friends. Knowing how she felt about me riding, there was no way Jack would ever let me use his bulls—if he knew about it.

Jana shook her head. "Dad won't be back from the High River rodeo till tomorrow, and Mom's gone shopping in Calgary."

"Sounds good," I said.

Terror leaned over to talk to Jana. "Okay if I take a few runs around the barrels?" she asked.

"Sure, Terr, help yourself. I'd like to see old Rambo run. Want to help me chase a couple of bulls in first?"

The girls got on their horses and rode into the corral behind the arena. I picked up my riggin' bag and walked into the cool dimness of the big building. I opened the gate that led into the chutes.

A minute later three bulls came trotting in. I knew the first two. They were Brahma crossed with some other breed and they weren't even two years old yet. Not too much of a challenge. I'd already ridden both of them.

But it was the third one that caught my eye. He was black and he had only one shiny black horn. That bull was no baby. He was full-grown and all Brahma. He had the big Brahma hump on his shoulders, the slippery loose hide over a body full of rippling muscle, and he definitely had the Brahma attitude. He had murder in his eyes.

Jana came loping up on Magpie, her pinto. "Sorry," she said. "I didn't mean to get old Rhino in there. He just saw the gate open and charged right in."

"Rhino?" I said.

"Yeah. The black guy. He broke his other horn off a few years ago. He's been Rhino ever since."

"Where'd he come from?" I asked. "I've never seen him before."

Jana laughed. "Oh, you know Dad. He's always trading. He just got Rhino from a stock contractor down south. He didn't take him to High River because he wanted the bull to settle down a little first." She started to turn her horse away. "I'll get him out of there," she said. "Which one do you want in the chute?"

"Him," I said.

"Who? Not Rhino."

"Yeah, him," I said, nodding toward the big black bull.

Jana reined Magpie to a sudden stop. "Hey, wait a minute…," she began, but I didn't let her finish.

"Come on, Jana, you know I'm not gonna learn any more from those young bulls. They're not tough enough."

Jana looked doubtful. "Yeah? And what if Rhino's too tough?"

I gave her a grin. "Then he's gonna win and I'm gonna lose. Let me try him, Jana. He looks like he's got the right attitude."

"He looks like he'll eat you for breakfast," Terror's voice cut in cheerfully from behind me. Good old Terror. Always looking out for her big brother's welfare.

I turned around and glared at her. "Don't get your hopes up, Terror. I'm gonna ride this sucker." I picked up my rope and headed for the chute.

The first thing I learned about Rhino was that he was a chute fighter. He wasn't planning to let me even get my rope on him. When I laid the rope across his back he gave a snort and started jumping around like he had a hide full of hornets. At that moment I wondered why anybody in his right mind would want to actually get on that bull. But, then again, who says bull riders are in their right mind anyway?

On the other side of the chute, Jana was getting the flank strap ready. She had been helping her dad with his rodeo stock since she was a little kid. She knew what she was doing.

Just like the name says, the flank strap goes around the bull's flanks. It's there to make him mad so he'll buck harder. It's not on for long and it doesn't hurt him, but it tickles enough to annoy him. It crossed my mind that old Rhino didn't seem to need any help in the getting-annoyed department, but we fastened the strap anyway.

Next came getting the rope around his belly just behind his front legs. The rope's pretty important because that's all the rider has to hang onto. Rhino finally stood still long enough for me to swing the rope underneath him. Jana caught it on the other side and pulled it up snug. She brought the tail of the rope up and tucked it through the handhold while I put my glove on my riding hand.

Rhino was roaring around in there again like an out-of-control bulldozer, and it took a couple of tries to carefully ease myself down onto his back. Instantly I felt the raw power rippling through his muscles. I could tell this was going to be some ride! I wondered what Dad would have thought of Rhino.

Jana's voice brought me back to the present. "Hurry up, Layne. Get that resin worked into your rope and let's get this show on the road. This bull isn't going to stand here much longer."

Personally, I had never noticed he was standing at all. Doing aerobics would be more like it. But Jana was right.

It was time to ride this bull. Quickly I slid my gloved hand up and down the rope. I could feel the resin I had worked into it warming up and getting sticky enough to keep my hand from slipping. I was almost ready.

"I don't know about this, Layne," Jana said, sounding worried. "Rhino's a pretty rank bull. What if he unloads you and then goes for you?"

I had sort of been wondering the same thing, but now I shrugged. "He's not so bad," I said. "He's just a chute fighter. He'll be okay when he gets outside. Besides," I added with a grin, "he's not gonna unload me."

Jana raised an eyebrow. "Think you're good, don't you?" she said, returning the grin.

"I know it."

She laughed out loud at that one. My macho act never has impressed Jana much. It didn't seem to impress the bull either. Right then he made a sudden lunge that almost mashed my leg against the gate. I settled down and paid attention to business.

Concentration. That's what it's all about. Dad used to say you rode bulls as much with your brain as with your body. Keep your mind in the middle and the rest of you will stay there too.

Okay, Dad, I thought. Watch this. I slid up on the rope, toes out, chin in. I took a deep breath and nodded. "Let him out!"

Jana jerked the gate open and got out of the way, fast.

Rhino exploded out of that chute and the whole world started spinning. In fact, the whole world disappeared. Everything was gone except for that bull and me. From what seemed like a million miles away I could hear a voice yelling, "Feet! Feet!" Somehow my mind took it in. Jana. Telling me to keep my feet in. Right. Feet in. Sit up straight. Pull hard on the rope. I tried to remember all the stuff Dad had told me. But that had been a long time ago…

Suddenly a flash of red caught my eye. Way up in the stands above the arena. Someone in a red shirt was up there watching. What were they doing there? Nobody else was supposed to be here. If someone told Mom about this I was dead.

It took maybe half a second for all of that to flash through my mind. But that was enough. I lost my concentration. My mind wasn't in the middle anymore. It was up there in the stands. And in that half second Rhino stopped spinning to the right. Then he was spinning to the left. I tried to shift my balance to go with him. But it was too late. I was losing it…

Chapter Three

I hit the ground hard and got the wind
knocked out of me. For a second
I was too stunned to think at all. Then a
feeling of relief swept over me. Rhino
had thrown me all right, but he'd thrown
me clear. I hadn't got hung up. Even as
I was thinking that, I was scrambling
to my feet. When you go off a bull you

don't stand around waiting to ask him if he'd enjoyed your company.

Apparently Rhino hadn't enjoyed mine. I caught one glimpse of black coming at me, and then I was flying through the air. I hit the soft ground face down and started trying to get up again. I had to get out of there fast. But it was too late. Before I could get up off my knees, Rhino's head slammed me back down. I knew I wasn't going to get away from him. It was time to play turtle.

I buried my head in my arms and pulled my knees up to my belly. Then he was after me again. I could feel the heat of his breath and smell the scent of hay on it. It smelled kind of good. Being killed by a bull probably beat being killed by a bear, I thought dimly. They say bears have rotten breath.

But they don't have horns, I reminded myself as I felt Rhino's single horn scrape across my ribs like a dull knife. If Rhino kept this up, he was going to spear something vital. I was surprised at how calm I felt. It was weird. I felt like I was far away, watching this happen. Like I wasn't a part of what was going on.

Suddenly, I heard someone yell, real close, and Rhino stopped trying to grind me into the dirt. I uncurled enough to glance up. What I saw scared me worse than being mauled by Rhino had. Terror was standing right in front of the bull, waving her jacket in his face and screaming at him. I tried to sit up, but before I could move the bull made up his mind. He gave a low bellow and went for Terror. Like lightning she jumped aside and he went charging by, tearing the jacket out of her hands.

He turned around, snorting and pawing the ground. But then Jana was there, charging in on her horse and swinging a big wicked whip in her hand. The end of it caught Rhino's glossy black rump with a loud smack. The bull gave a startled bawl and instantly forgot Terror and me. He turned and galloped with Jana and Magpie right behind him. Jana chased him on out the side gate.

I propped myself up on one elbow and spit out some dirt. I looked up at Terror. She was standing there grinning like she was in her right mind. "Of all the stupid, pea-brained, airheaded…," I began, but I was still crunching sand between my teeth. I spit out some more and tried again. "What were you tryin' to do? Get killed?" I yelled. My voice came out kind of shaky. Actually I was starting to feel kind of shaky all over.

Terror just shrugged. "Look who's talkin' about tryin' to get killed. At least I'm not bleeding."

"What's that got to do with anything?" I asked impatiently.

"Well," she said calmly, "you *are* bleeding."

"I am?" I said, surprised. So far I'd been too busy taking a strip off her to worry about me. But now I looked down and saw a big rip in the side of my shirt. Around it the torn edges of the faded denim were slowly turning dark red. Now that I thought about it, my side was starting to hurt some too. I pulled out my shirttail and checked the damage. There was a long, bloody groove across my ribs—thanks to Rhino's one sharp horn. It was a messy-looking cut, but I didn't think it was deep enough to be serious.

I looked up, ready to tell Terror that the cut was nothing. That's when I noticed the man walking slowly across the arena. My first reaction to him was anger. This was the guy in the red shirt, the one I'd seen up in the stands. He was the reason I had lost my concentration.

If it hadn't been for him I would have ridden Rhino—maybe.

The man was close enough to recognize now. That led to my second reaction, a sinking feeling in the pit of my stomach. It was Chase Kincaid, Jana's grandfather, and I figured he was going to have a few questions.

What did I think I was doing riding Jack Kelvin's bulls without permission? That would probably be the first question. Unfortunately, I didn't have a real good answer handy.

Jana finished locking up the bull and rode over to see what was happening. She and Chase got there at about the same time. For a minute nobody said anything. Chase just stood there glaring at all three of us with those pale old eagle eyes of his. I stood there scuffing my boots in the dirt and waiting for him to start yelling. The silence stretched out.

Finally I heard Jana take a deep breath. "Uh, hi, Gramps," she said with a sick smile. "I, uh, thought you went with Mom. But I guess you didn't 'cause you're, uh, here…"

Shut up, Jana, I said silently. When you're in this deep, every word just gets you in deeper. But Jana isn't a very good mind reader. She kept right on talking. "Uh, Gramps, this is a friend of mine, Layne McQueen. You know, he lives…"

She didn't get a chance to finish. Chase finally spoke up, cutting her off. "'Course I know who he is. I remember the day he was born. Never saw a man prouder than Jeff McQueen was that day."

I stood there staring at him. The last thing I'd expected was for him to start talking about Dad. But I guess they had known each other pretty well. Dad used to talk about Chase a lot. Chase had been a bull rider too. Not just a bull rider, I remembered. According to Dad, he had been the best.

But just when I was beginning to hope that Chase had got lost somewhere in the past, his eagle eyes focused on me. "But what I don't know," he said slowly, "is what you think you're tryin' to do here."

I swallowed hard and prepared to die. "I was practicing," I said weakly.

Chase gave kind of a snort. "Well, from what I could see, Lord knows you could use the practice."

I felt my face turning red. Being caught riding Kelvin's bulls was bad enough. Being told I was lousy didn't make me feel any better.

Chase went on. "Don't suppose you ever thought of walking up like a man and asking when you want to use something. Or is sneaking around always your style?"

I had that coming. "No, sir, it isn't usually my style. I'm sorry. I should've known better," I added, wishing I were dead and buried.

Chase nodded. "Yeah," he said. He thought a minute. Then he pushed back his hat and gave me a puzzled look. "So," he said at last, "if you're so all-fired set on riding bulls, why don't you just sign up for the next rodeo like all the other guys?"

I hated answering that question. I studied my boots. "My mom won't let me," I muttered. It made me feel like I was too young to cross the street alone.

Chase thought that over for a minute. What he said next surprised me. "On account of what happened to your dad?" he asked gently.

I nodded. "How'd you know?" I asked, giving Jana an accusing look. She was about the only person who knew why I couldn't ride bulls at rodeos.

Chase had only come back to live here a couple of months ago, so he wouldn't know unless someone had told him.

But maybe Chase hadn't needed an explanation. "It's a natural enough reaction," he said. "I don't blame your mom." Sure, I thought. He'd be on her side. But then he added, "Don't blame you either."

I was still taking that in when I made the mistake of reaching over to rub my sore ribs. Chase noticed the blood. "Cut you up a little, huh?" he said. I nodded. Right then I was a lot more interested in what he meant by that last comment. But I wasn't about to find out. Chase stepped forward for a closer look. "Let's see," he ordered.

He leaned over and inspected the cut. "Hmm," he muttered, reaching into his pocket and coming out with a jackknife. I almost backed up. What was this? Instant surgery while you wait? But it was just my shirttail he was after. He cut off a chunk. "Shirt's done for anyway," he said. He pulled a fairly clean old bandana handkerchief out of his pocket and slapped it on the cut. "Here, hold this," he ordered. I did and he wrapped the strip of shirt around me to hold the handkerchief in place. Then he jerked it real tight. I winced as it bit into my ribs.

Chase gave me a sharp look. "You all right?" he asked.

I nodded. "Yeah, I'm okay," I said. Bull riding injuries come in two kinds. If you're moving, you're okay. If you're not, they get the stretcher.

I was definitely okay.

Chapter Four

There was no point in hanging around any longer. It was only going to be a matter of time before Chase told Jana's parents and they told Mom. I could feel his eyes on me as I turned away. Head down, I started walking out to the truck. Jana fell into step beside me.

"You look kind of pale," she said worriedly. "You sure you feel okay, Layne?"

"Yeah," I began, meaning to say, "It was nothin'." But then I looked up into Jana's big brown eyes. They were soft and full of concern—and real pretty. I began to take a turn for the worse. "Well," I said, trying to sound brave but in pain, "I guess I could be better. I'm kinda shook."

It worked. Jana reached out and put her arm around my waist. "Here," she said. "Lean on me." I did and we walked over to the truck. I was feeling better already.

Terror was walking beside us, leading the horses. She caught my eye once and the look on her face said she was ready to either laugh or throw up. I couldn't decide which. Sometimes my kid sister sees through me a little too well.

Luckily, it was right then that Rambo decided to reach over and take a bite out of Magpie's neck. Magpie went straight up and Terror had all she could handle sorting out that little rodeo. At least it got her mind off my business. Maybe old Rambo really did have his good side.

We got him loaded without too much trouble. Then I started to climb in on the driver's side. Terror stopped me. "Hey, Layne, since you're feeling 'kinda shook,' maybe I should drive."

"Dream on, kid," I said, sliding behind the wheel. "You're only twelve."

She shrugged. "Never hurts to try," she said, walking around to the other side.

Jana stood leaning on my door. "I'm really sorry, Layne," she said softly. "I should have double-checked to be sure Gramps wasn't home."

"Hey," I said, grinning to make her feel better, "it's not your fault. I probably would have got caught sooner or later anyhow."

"What's your mom gonna say?"

I sighed. "Don't ask."

Jana just stood there giving me that worried look for a minute. Then, suddenly, she leaned over and gave me a quick kiss. "Good luck, Layne," she said.

"Oh, gross," Terror muttered, and I felt my face start to burn. Still, the kiss had been worth it. It almost made up for everything that had gone wrong today. Almost.

"Thanks, Jana," I said real low. "For everything."

As we drove out of the yard I got one last glimpse of Chase. He was leaning on the fence watching us go. I couldn't read the expression on his face.

We drove in silence for a while. Finally I glanced over at Terror. "So," I said wearily, "I suppose you can't wait to blab the whole story to Mom."

She gave me a narrow-eyed look. "Well, isn't that what you'd expect from a stupid, pea-brained, airheaded—"

I cut her off. "Okay, okay, I didn't mean that stuff. But you had me so scared…"

Terror fluffed up like an angry cat. "I had *you* scared?" she squeaked. "If somebody hadn't done something, that bull would have made hamburger out of you!"

I couldn't come up with a real good answer to that. I couldn't actually think of much to say at all. Except for one thing. And it wasn't going to be easy. "Uh, Terr?" She looked at me. "What you did, about the bull I mean, that was real brave." Talking nice to Terror was something I hadn't practiced much, and I was stumbling around to find the right words. But what I said next just came out. "Dad would have been proud of you."

She sat up straight and stared at me, eyes wide. "You really think so?" she said.

I smiled. "Sure," I said. And right then she started to cry.

I couldn't believe it. Terror never cried. And I didn't know she ever even thought much about Dad. She'd only been six when he died. I reached over and gave her a one-armed hug. "Hey, what's the matter? I was tryin' to say somethin' nice to you."

She nodded and sniffed a couple of times and just sat there leaning on my shoulder for a minute. Then in a small voice she said, "I know. It's just that when Rhino went after you it seemed like it was all gonna happen again. I don't want to lose you too, Layne."

I swallowed. "Nothin's gonna happen to me, Terr."

Right then the front wheel hit a pothole and the trailer did a little fishtail behind us. Terror shook off my arm and sat up straight. "Something will if you keep drivin' like that. Pay attention. You're shakin' up my horse."

I smiled and put my hand back on the wheel. The real Terror was back.

Neither of us said anything the rest of the way home. Then, as we started up the driveway, Terror turned to me. "You never know," she said. "Maybe Chase won't tell."

"Sure," I said, "and maybe I'm Arnold Schwarzenegger."

After supper I made a halfhearted stab at doing my homework. Terror turned on the TV, but I decided to go to bed early. I was feeling like I'd been run over by a bull. And that was nothing compared to how I expected to feel once

Mom found out. I didn't think I'd be able to sleep, but the next thing I knew it was morning.

I woke up to the sound of a quick knock on my bedroom door. I blinked, tried to sit up fast and got a stab of pain through my ribs for my trouble. The door opened and there was Mom, gathering up my dirty clothes to wash.

"Mornin', Sunshine," she said brightly, throwing a teasing grin over her shoulder. It was an old joke between us. Sunshine was one name that didn't exactly fit me first thing in the morning.

"Mornin'," I muttered sleepily, trying to sort some things out in my mind. Remembering the fight I'd had with her yesterday, I was surprised at her good mood. She probably thought that she'd won that little set-to. Now she wanted to show there were no hard feelings about it. Okay, Mom, I thought. No hard feelings. But you still haven't won.

Right in the middle of that thought I saw something that brought my attention back to the present real fast. My denim shirt, the one with the rip and the blood, was lying crumpled up in the corner right where I'd tossed it last night. I'd been meaning to get rid of it first thing in the morning, but now it was too late. Sure enough, Mom spotted it.

She shook her head. "You are some housekeeper, Layne," she muttered as she bent over to pick it up. "Ever think of putting your dirty clothes in the hamper?" She gave the shirt a shake and started to throw it in the basket. Then she took another look.

When she looked up at me there was a little crease between her eyes. That usually means she's either thinking hard or getting mad. Sometimes both. "Now what…?" she began. I wasn't sure if she expected an answer from me. She didn't get one anyway. Like the cops always say on TV, "You have the right to remain silent. Anything you say may be held against you…"

She focused her stern look on me. "Did you have rugby practice after school?" she asked, sounding disgusted.

That was the last question I expected and it caught me off guard. "Uh, yeah," I answered honestly. She should have known that I did. I was late getting home because of it. But I still didn't know what that had to do with anything.

I soon found out though. "Well, for two cents I'd phone up that coach of yours and give him a piece of my mind. This is the third shirt you've ruined this month. Why you can't remember to take along an old sweatshirt on practice days is more than I know. And look at this," she went on. "Blood even. You're always getting scratched up. That rugby is too violent for a bunch of schoolkids."

She finally ran out of steam, and I let out a little sigh of relief. Wow! That had been a close one. I said a mental thank-you to Mr. Bowlen and his killer rugby practices. He didn't know it, but he had just saved my neck—temporarily at least. There was still the problem of Chase Kincaid hanging over me.

Then I realized that Mom was still muttering about rugby. The way she was going on I was beginning to think she really would phone Mr. Bowlen.

I sat up a little straighter, making sure to take the blanket with me. I still had on Chase's homemade bandage. I didn't think Mom would buy the idea that it had come from the school first aid kit. "You know," I said innocently, "I'm gettin' kinda sick of rugby. Maybe I'll take up a different sport."

Mom gave me a suspicious look. I guess I'd never given up that easily before in my life. But, luckily, she was too busy to worry about it. She stuffed the shirt in the basket and headed for the door. "Good idea, Layne," she said over her shoulder. "Anything would be an improvement."

I smiled as she went out the door. "Anything, Mom?" I said quietly.

Chapter Five

I didn't have a great day at school. With everything that had happened I'd accidentally-on-purpose forgotten to do my homework. That got me an after-school detention. I spent the whole day with that hanging over me. But that was nothing compared to thinking about what would be waiting for me when

I got home from school. I figured that, by then, Chase would have spilled the beans to Mom. Compared to going home, the detention was starting to look kind of good.

I had to walk home, but we don't live too far out of town so that wasn't so bad. It was about four thirty when I turned into our lane. Nobody was in sight. That was a relief. I'd been half expecting Mom to be at the door, waiting to ambush me.

I opened the door and walked into the house. Still no sign of Mom. Just Terror eating peanut butter with a spoon and watching *The Young and the Restless*. I dumped my books on the table. "Where's Mom?" I asked.

Terror ignored me until the couple on the screen finished kissing. Then she set the peanut butter down and looked in my direction. "Out," she said helpfully.

"I know she's out. Out where?"

Terror shrugged. "Checking on the cows, I think." Then, acting real innocent, she asked, "Why do you want to know?"

"You know why I want to know," I shot back impatiently. "So what's she acting like? Did she find out?"

Another shrug. "She didn't say anything."

The show ended. Terror turned the TV off. "Oh, yeah," she said casually. "You had a phone call."

"I did? Who was it? Jana?"

"Nope."

"Well, who?" I asked, my voice rising. I could wring her neck when she takes her mysterious streaks.

"Chase Kincaid," she said, giving me a sideways look.

That hit me like a punch in the stomach. "Chase! Did he talk to Mom?"

Terror shook her head. "She was outside. Anyway, it was you he wanted."

For a minute I just stood there trying to take that in. I wondered if this was good news or bad. Before I could decide, Terror went on. "He left you a message."

"Yeah? What'd he say?"

"He said to show up at the arena tonight at seven."

"And bring Mom?" I asked kind of sickly.

Terror shook her head. "No. He asked what time Mom went to work. I said six. That's when he said seven."

I stared at her for a minute, wondering if she was making all this up. It was pretty weird. "Well," I demanded, "what else did he say?"

Terror picked up an apple and bit into it with a loud crunch. "Nothin'," she said. "Except that I could come too if I wanted." She opened the door and then stopped. "So," she asked, "are you gonna show up?"

I sighed. "I don't think I've got a choice," I said. Whatever game Chase was playing, he was holding all the aces.

Mom came in after a while. She just acted normal so I tried to do the same. Whatever Chase had in mind, I decided he hadn't said anything to her yet. I wasn't looking forward to facing him, but the suspense was killing me. It seemed like Mom would never leave for work. When she finally did, I spent the next three-quarters of an hour pacing.

At six forty-five I was in the truck. So was Terror. I didn't really want her along, but I was in no position to give her static.

The first thing I noticed when we drove into Kelvins' yard was that both the vehicles were missing. Jana's mom and dad must be away again. Jana was there though. She came out to meet us.

"Hi, Jana," I said nervously. "What's goin' on?"

Jana looked as confused as I felt. "Beats me. Gramps just mentioned that you might be coming over. That's all he said."

I didn't get a chance for any more questions. Chase was strolling over from the arena. I noticed that he limped a little. Most old bull riders do.

I got out of the truck and stood there waiting. Chase gave me a long, measuring look. "How you feelin'?" he asked at last.

That wasn't what I'd been expecting. For a second my mind went blank. He'd called me over here to ask about my health? What did that have to do with anything? Then it sunk in. The last Chase had seen of me, Rhino had just finished scrubbing the arena floor with me. I hadn't been in the best of health right then. "I'm okay," I said kind of sheepishly.

Chase nodded. "Good," he said. "Where's your bull rope?"

I stared at him. "In the truck," I said. I always kept it behind the seat so Mom wouldn't find it. But what did Chase want with it? Was he going to take it away from me so I couldn't sneak any more rides?

"Get it," Chase said. I did. Then he turned to Jana. "Go and saddle up a horse." He glanced at Terror. "Get one for the bullfighter here too," he added.

"Okay, Gramps," Jana said, giving him an unbelieving look. "Come on, Terr."

The look on Terror's face almost made me grin. She doesn't usually take orders. She did this time though. There was something about Chase Kincaid that said you didn't cross him. A little late for you to figure that out, Layne, I thought bitterly. I figured I'd already crossed him pretty good.

"Here," I muttered, holding my bull rope out to him. I was remembering how long it had taken to save the money to buy it.

Chase didn't take the rope. He just gave me a scornful look. "What're you givin' me that for? Think I'm about to climb on a bull at my age?"

I stared at him. "No, but you said—"

He cut me off. "I said get it. Now you've got it."

Without another word he limped off toward the arena. I just stood there until he threw me an impatient glance over his shoulder. "Well," he said, "are you comin' or ain't you?"

Good question, I thought. It would help if I knew where we were going and why. Chase had kept me off balance from the minute I drove in. I was getting kind of sick of being jerked around like a lassoed calf. But I followed him.

Just as I caught up with him, Jana and Terror rode up on a couple of Jana's horses. "Now what, Gramps?" Jana asked.

"Go run in a couple of the young bulls," Chase ordered.

Jana just looked at him. "Got a hearing problem?" Chase asked, giving her his "eagle" look.

Suddenly, Jana grinned. "No sir!" she yelled. "Come on, Terr!" They took off at a gallop.

That left Chase and me. I figured we'd played enough games for one day. "You gonna tell me what's goin' on?" I matched his glare with one of my own.

Chase took his time answering. First he brought a can of Copenhagen out of his back pocket and helped himself to a chew. He didn't offer me any. Then he nodded to the rope in my hand. "Suppose I took that thing away from you, told your mom what you'd been up to and told you to stay away from the bulls. What would you do?"

I didn't take time to think about the answer. If I had, maybe I wouldn't have told the truth. But the words just came out. "I'd get another rope, and I'd find another place to practice, and if Mom couldn't handle it I'd find another place to live."

It was the first time I'd realized how important this was to me. But once I'd said it I knew I meant every word. I guess Chase knew I meant it too. He nodded.

"That's what I figured," he said gruffly, but his lined face had softened a little. "So," he added, "if you're gonna do it, you might just as well do it right as wrong."

Slowly I began to understand. "You mean you're gonna teach me?" I asked.

"Depends if you're teachable," Chase said. Something pretty close to a grin was creeping across his face.

I didn't know what to say. Being taught by the guy Dad had said was the best bull rider he'd ever known? It was like Christmas had come seven months early. "I'll learn," I promised. "I'll do whatever you say."

Chase nodded. "We'll see," he said. "But there's one thing," he added. "This is just between us four—you, me and the girls. If your mom or Jana's parents find out, we're all in trouble."

"Okay," I said. "I'm sure not about to tell anybody." Then, as the bulls came trotting in, I had to ask one last question. "Chase? You're really stickin' your neck out for me. Why?"

Chase thought a minute. "I remember how tough it was bein' a kid," he said at last. "You want to do something so bad, but nobody thinks you're old enough to handle it." He turned and started walking toward the chutes. Then, over his shoulder, he added, "There's only one thing worse. That's bein' so old nobody thinks you can do anything."

He kept on walking, but I had my answer.

Chapter Six

I watched as Chase picked out the bull
he wanted. I didn't understand the
choice he made. It was a pretty good-
sized bull for its age all right, big-boned
and well-muscled. But from its red and
white color and mellow disposition I'd
have bet this bull had more Hereford
than Brahma in him.

I climbed up on the fence beside Chase. "I've ridden him before," I said. "He's not much of a bull."

Chase swept a cold glance in my direction. "Well, ride him again," he said. Something in his voice told me not to argue.

We got the rigging on the bull and I slid on. Chase leaned over me, making adjustments and giving advice. He pulled my rope snug for me, and I started to weave it in and out of my fingers like I always did. Suddenly Chase's hand clamped onto my wrist like an eagle's claw would grab a rabbit. "What do you think you're doin'?" he asked in a voice as hard as his grip.

I just stared at him, stunned. "What do you mean?" I asked.

He still didn't let go of my wrist. "Don't you know any better than to use a suicide wrap?"

"Suicide wrap?" I repeated.

Chase nodded grimly. "Yeah. That's what it's called and that's what it is. You fall off wrong with your hand tied in like that and you're dead. Whoever taught you that should be shot. Who was it, anyhow?" he demanded, his eyes burning into me.

I looked back at him defiantly. "My dad," I said.

There was a silence. Then Chase nodded. "It figures," he said wearily.

I almost shot back an angry reply. I didn't know what that comment was supposed to mean, but I didn't like it. Nobody put my dad down when I was around. But then the truth began to sink in. Dad had always ridden with a "suicide wrap"—and now Dad was dead. In all the years since the accident I'd never really put it together.

Chase's soft voice interrupted my thoughts. "Yeah," he said, "some guys figure that the extra grip it gives you is worth the risk. But as long as you're workin' with me you ain't gonna be one of them." Before I could argue he was rearranging the rope, running it through my gloved hand. Then he folded the tail of the rope back over—but without weaving it between my fingers.

I flexed my hand. It felt funny that way. I gave Chase an angry look. He ignored it. "Ready?" he asked. I nodded. He climbed down, and a second later the chute gate was flung open.

The bull plunged out of the chute, and I was in trouble from the first jump. It wasn't because he was bucking all that great. When I rode him before, I didn't have any trouble staying on. No, the bull wasn't the problem. I was. I was all out of rhythm with him. It was all wrong. He gave a jump and a twist in the opposite direction...

I hit the dirt hard—and scrambled to my feet a split second later. Rhino had taught me what happened if you lay around too long. But I didn't need to worry. This bull was no fighter. He was already trotting toward the gate Jana was holding open for him. I thought he had kind of a bull-grin on his face.

Disgustedly, I brushed the dirt off my clothes and picked up my hat. Head down, I trudged back to Chase. I could feel his eyes on me, but I wouldn't look at him. Instead, I bent over and tightened a spur strap.

Chase's voice finally broke the silence. "Well, what did you learn from that experience?"

I shrugged. "I dunno," I muttered.

"Yes, you do. You weren't concentrating. Your mind wasn't on the bull. It was on how mad you were at me."

I fought back. "I could've rode him—my way."

"You might have stayed on him your way. A halfway bright chimpanzee might have stayed on him too. It would take a cowboy to learn to do it right. And I guess you aren't interested." Chase turned and started walking away.

I watched him. Half of me was glad to see him go. Let him find some other sucker to boss around. I didn't need anything from some old washed-up cowboy. But the other half of me wasn't so sure. Somewhere, deep down and well buried, I had a good idea that Chase was right. I had as much to unlearn as I had to learn. And the first thing I was going to have to learn was to swallow my pride. I started after him.

"Chase?"

He stopped walking. I caught up. "So, uh, can I try another one?" We looked at each other for a few long seconds. "Your way," I added quietly.

Chase hesitated. Then, slowly, something close to a smile spread across his weathered face. He reached out and laid an arm across my shoulders. "Okay," he said, "let's go pick one out, cowboy."

Chapter Seven

The next few weeks went by in a blur. I spent every possible minute down at the arena, practicing. I spent so much time sneaking around avoiding both Mom and Jana's parents that sometimes I felt like a secret agent.

Mom and I were getting along great. That didn't make me feel any better about the way I was going behind her back, but I couldn't help it. I had to ride.

At least all that illegal practice was doing some good. Chase made a point of grumping and growling at me a lot just to keep me in line. I could tell he thought I was improving though. He'd actually let me move up to riding the full-grown bulls when they weren't away at a rodeo. By the end of three weeks I'd tried them all—except one.

I finished unbuckling my spurs after a ride one night and looked up at Chase. "So why won't you let me try him again?" I asked.

Chase knew what I was talking about. He gave me a level look. "'Cause you aren't ready for Rhino yet."

Getting mad at Chase never did get me anywhere, but sometimes I'm a real slow learner. I got mad again. "Well, when am I gonna be ready? Next year?"

Chase shrugged. "Maybe. What are you in such an all-fired hurry about?"

I shrugged back. "Nothin'. I just want to ride him. That's all."

That was part of the truth. Enough truth to get by with. But I hadn't counted on a little help from Terror, who was hanging around as usual. "Yeah," she put in. "He wants to prove to himself that he can do it 'cause he entered the rodeo two weeks from now."

Chase gave me a sharp look. "That right?" he demanded.

I glared at Terror. I'd been meaning to tell Chase when the time was right. It sure didn't seem right now. "Yeah," I admitted. "I entered even before you started helping me."

"And what do you figure your mother's gonna say?"

I sighed. That was a real good question. It was one I'd already asked myself about a thousand times. "I don't know," I said wearily. "But she's gonna have to find out sometime."

"You got that right," Chase said and walked away before I could decide what he was thinking.

With the rodeo getting this close, it was on my mind all the time. I could hardly even eat for worrying about it. I was halfheartedly shoveling in my meatloaf one night when Mom came up with a big announcement. "Guess what," she said.

"What?" Terror asked instantly. If my kid sister were a cat, curiosity would have killed her a long time ago.

"Your cousin Becky is getting married."

"Oh, gross!" Terror squawked. "Who'd want to marry Becky?"

It was one of the few times I could remember when Terror and I agreed.

Becky was about three years older than me, but it seemed more like thirty-three. She lived in Edmonton and always acted like we were some kind of savages because we lived in the country. The few times she had come to visit had been some of the worst days of my life. She'd spent most of her time tippy-toeing around the barnyard like a ballet dancer, squealing if she happened to step in a little horse manure. I was glad she was getting married. Maybe she'd move to Egypt or somewhere.

Mom ignored Terror's outburst. "And," she continued, "we're all invited."

"I'm not going," Terror announced.

"Me neither," I added, even though it meant agreeing with Terror.

Mom sighed and shook her head, but she was almost smiling. "I had a feeling it might be that way," she said. "Well, I'm not about to drag either one of you, but Becky's my only niece and I'm not going to pass up her wedding. After all," she added, giving Terror a teasing grin, "if my daughter ever gets married she'll probably want to do it in a barn with her horse for a bridesmaid."

Terror shook her head violently. "No way, Mom! Rambo's a boy. He'll have to be the best man."

Mom just shook her head. "Okay, I give up. But if you two stay home, you'll be in charge of the chores."

"Sure," I said, happy to get off so easy. "When is it?"

"July third."

July third? That had a familiar sound. Suddenly I knew why. That was the first day of the rodeo. And if Mom was in Edmonton...

I glanced across the table and caught Terror's eye. She winked. Yeah. It was all working out perfectly.

With everything falling into place like that, I couldn't wait to get in some more practice. I had to wait though. It was three days later when Jana phoned to say that the coast was finally clear. She said to hurry because she wasn't sure how long her parents would be gone. I think I might have set the world's land speed record driving over there.

When I walked into the arena, Chase already had a bull in the chute. I could hear it banging around in there before I could see it. Then my eyes adjusted to the dimness of the arena and I saw the big black body. The bull threw up his head and I caught the dull gleam of a black horn. Just one horn. It was rematch time. Me and Rhino. A cold shiver suddenly ran through me. I walked faster.

"He's all ready to go, huh?" I asked Chase.

Chase nodded. "Oh, yeah, he's real ready. Are you?" he asked, studying my face.

"Sure. Why wouldn't I be?"

"No reason. Let's get this show on the road. We haven't got all day. Jana, you keep an eye out that window and watch for your dad. He didn't say when he'd be back."

"Okay, Gramps," Jana said, but it looked like she was more interested in keeping an eye on me. "Be careful, Layne," she said and paused like she wanted to say something more.

I didn't give her the chance. "Sure," I said, managing a grin. "Ain't I always?"

"No," she shot back and turned to look out the window.

I climbed up on the side of the chute to help Chase get the rigging on the bull. One thing was for sure. Rhino was still a chute fighter. He was rank in there, tossing his head and banging that one horn against the gate. I wished he would quit. It was getting on my nerves. There was something else too. The way he kept watching me. Even while he was crashing around it seemed like he had his eyes rolled back, watching every move I made. It was like he remembered me. Did he remember how close he'd come to killing me? Was he planning to try again?

Chase was talking to me, giving me advice or instructions or something, but I kept tuning out. I was watching Rhino watch me. "Well, come on," Chase's voice finally came through to me. "Get down on him and let's get him outside before he tears the chute apart."

"Huh? Oh, yeah sure," I mumbled. I climbed over the top plank and carefully started lowering myself onto

Rhino's back. My stomach was doing cartwheels. I settled my weight on the bull and slowly started sliding up on my rope. I could feel Rhino's muscles under me. I swallowed hard, wishing I'd skipped supper. Rhino whipped his head around sideways, trying to hook my leg. He gave a low threatening bawl. I was sweating.

Chase laid a firm hand on my shoulder. "Layne," he asked, his voice gentle for him, "you sure you're ready for this?"

I pulled down my hat and took a deep breath. "Yeah," I said, somehow keeping my voice level. "I'm sure. Come on. Turn him out!"

Chase climbed down. He was reaching for the gate rope when Jana's yell stopped him. "Hey, you guys! Dad's truck just came around the corner!"

I swore softly as I climbed off the bull and onto the chute fence. I was the only one who knew it was from pure relief.

"Too bad, kid," Chase said, disgusted. "Let's get this bull put away fast. You and him will have to wait till next time."

"Yeah," I said as I pulled my rope off Rhino. "That's a real rip-off."

Chase opened the back gate, and I watched Rhino trot into the corral with the other bulls. It was a full hour later when my hands finally stopped shaking.

It turned out that Rhino and I didn't get together again. The next time Jana's parents were away at a rodeo, they took Rhino with them. I had to settle for riding the young bulls again. Then, on the way home from the rodeo, Rhino got his foot stepped on. He came out of the truck limping and bleeding.

Nobody would be riding him for a while. Maybe he'd never be a bucking bull again, I thought. Maybe there was just a lot of baloney in his future. I tried to feel bad about that, but didn't have much luck.

Chapter Eight

July 3 dawned hot and sunny. A perfect rodeo day. I couldn't wait to get Mom out of the house, but she took her time. I paced around like a caged tiger while she fixed her hair and her fingernails and her eyelashes. "You're gonna be late, Mom," I nagged.

She laughed at me. "It doesn't take five hours to get to Edmonton even at the speed you think I drive." At last she gathered up her purse and headed for the door. Then she stopped and dug out her wallet. She handed me a fifty-dollar bill. "Here, this'll get you and Tara into the rodeo and give you some left over to take Jana on some rides on the midway. You kids are going to the rodeo, aren't you?"

I nodded without looking her in the eye. Don't do this to me, Mom, I thought. Don't be nice to me when I'm pulling a rotten trick on you.

"Well, come on then, Sunshine. Lighten up and take the money. You deserve it for staying home and doing all the chores for me." Reluctantly, I took the fifty.

"Bye, Mom," I said.

"Bye, Layne. See you tonight. Tell your sister goodbye for me. She's disappeared somewhere with that Rambo horse. Don't let her break her neck, will you?" Mom jumped in the car and roared off in a cloud of dust. Feeling guilty, I stuffed the money in my pocket and went inside to change my clothes.

When I came out, Terror was just leading Rambo out of the barn. "Hey, you better put that horse away and get ready if you're comin' with me," I said. "The rodeo starts in an hour."

"I am ready. We just have to load Rambo."

I stared at her. "We have to *what*?"

"You heard me. I entered him in the barrel racing."

"You *what*?" I sputtered. "You entered that crazy horse in the barrel racing without Mom's permission? If she knew that she'd wring your neck..."

For once Terror didn't interrupt me. She just let me keep right on talking— until I'd talked myself in so deep that even I realized what I'd done. I sighed and added, "Just like she'd wring my neck if she knew what I'm doing."

Terror smiled. "Ready to load Rambo?" she asked sweetly.

We loaded him. He bit a chunk out of my sleeve while we were doing it. That didn't improve my mood much. But at last he was in the trailer. "Get in!" I yelled at Terror. "We're runnin' out of time."

She walked around to the passenger side. Suddenly, I heard her groan. "Oh, no!"

I jumped out of the truck. "Now what?" I yelled. Terror just pointed at the flat tire on the horse trailer.

I slammed my fist against the side of the trailer. "Well, that does it! That really does it! There's no spare, and I don't have time to fix that tire. Sorry, Terr. Rambo stays home."

I waited for Terror to explode. But she didn't. She just stood there staring at her dusty boots for a minute. Then she nodded. "Okay, Layne," she said in a real low voice. As she turned to open the trailer door I saw her wipe her hand across her eyes. I got a real rotten feeling in the pit of my stomach. Terror must have wanted this chance real bad. I knew how that felt.

I glanced at the truck. While the trailer was in the repair shop last month we had put the old stock racks on the truck to haul some calves. The racks were still on. We'd used them to haul horses before. "Terr?"

"What?"

"Go lead Rambo up the loading ramp. We'll haul him in the truck."

The look on Terror's face was worth the fifteen minutes I was going to lose. I unhitched the trailer and backed the truck up to the ramp.

Rambo wasn't real impressed with the idea of walking into the back of the truck. He reared up and pawed the air a couple of times. Once he just missed clipping my ear with a front hoof. "Wow!" Terror said. "That looked neat. Just like a wild stallion in the movies." What I said at that point wasn't quite so pleasant.

At last he was in, and I eased the truck away from the ramp. Rambo was restless. As we started down the lane I could feel the truck sway as he shifted his weight from side to side. I was glad it was only fifteen minutes to the rodeo grounds.

I pulled out onto the main road, being careful not to turn too sharp and throw the horse off balance. He seemed to be settling down a little. Then I caught a flash of red in the rearview mirror. It was Rick Barker's old Camaro. Rick was the school's number one party animal, and I could see that he had a whole carload of his crazy buddies with him. They were doing way over the speed limit so I pulled over to let them go by. As he started to pass, Rick leaned on the horn. Heads leaned out all four windows. "YAHOO!" they all howled.

I felt the whole truck lurch. The outside mirror gave me one glimpse of Rambo's big body rearing to its full height. There was a splintering crash as he went over the side of the stock rack.

"No!" I heard Terror's choked gasp. Then she was piling out of the truck before I could even get it completely stopped.

By the time I got there, Terror was kneeling in the ditch beside Rambo. I could see that he was alive. I didn't know if that was good news or bad.

Silently, I knelt beside her. "I'm sorry, Terr," I whispered.

This time she really was crying and not trying to hide it. "It wasn't your fault," she said between sobs. "It was those, those…" She ran out of words, but I could have filled in plenty of them for her. Rick and his friends hadn't even stopped.

I took a closer look at Rambo. One front leg was streaming blood. Outside of that I couldn't see any cuts on him. But I didn't know what might be broken. Carefully, I ran a hand down the bleeding leg. There was a wicked cut in the muscle above the knee, but I couldn't feel any broken bones. Maybe, just maybe… No, I told myself. A horse couldn't take a fall like that and come out of it with just a cut.

Suddenly, Rambo began to struggle. He threw his head up and tried to get his feet under him. I dragged Terror out of the way of the scrambling hoofs. Then, unbelievably, Rambo was on his feet. He was swaying kind of drunkenly and not putting any weight on the injured leg. But he was up. He had a chance!

I was running for the truck. "Hang in there, Terr! I'm gonna call the vet."

Five minutes later the vet was on his way and I was back with Terror and Rambo. The horse was still on his feet. Terror was holding his head against her as if she could give him the strength he needed to survive. She turned her tear-stained face toward me. "You go and ride your bull, Layne," she said softly. "Me and Rambo will be okay until the vet comes." She really meant it.

I shook my head. "Forget it, Terr. The bull's not important." That was a lie. The bull was really important. But right now what happened to my kid sister and her horse was a lot more important.

The vet took his time going over Rambo. It didn't help any that Rambo kept trying to bite him. But I took that as a sign that Rambo was starting to act fairly normal. Finally, the vet finished and shook his head in amazement.

"That's quite a horse you've got there, Tara. Aside from that nasty cut, a lot of bruises and a pretty fair case of shock, I can't find anything wrong with him. I'll send my wife out with our trailer. You take him home, keep him warm and quiet overnight, and then let him rest till that leg heals. He'll live to fight again—likely even barrel race again."

"He ain't called Rambo for nothin'," Terror said proudly. A huge grin of relief spread across her face.

It was almost five o'clock when we finally got Rambo home and bedded down in the barn. The rodeo was over for the day and my chance to ride there was over for another year. Then I thought of something else. In a few hours Mom would be home. I'd expected that I'd be in trouble when she found out that I'd ridden a bull. Well, I hadn't ridden one and I was still going to be in a whole pile of trouble. I could imagine Mom's reaction when she found out about Rambo. Yeah, this day had been bad, but it was going to get worse.

The phone rang and I jumped. My nerves were really shot. I reached for it. "Hello?"

It was Mom. "Hi," she said, sounding happy. "How's everything with you guys?"

"Fine," I said. She might as well stay happy for a while longer. She'd get unhappy fast enough when she got home.

"Did you have fun at the rodeo this afternoon?"

"Yeah, it was a pretty exciting afternoon." I was getting good at not telling the truth without actually lying.

"Oh, good. I was feeling kind of guilty having a good time here without you kids. And now Aunt Bonnie really wants me to stay over until tomorrow. You think you guys can manage if I do?"

"Sure, Mom," I said tiredly. "No sweat."

"You're sure everything's okay?" Mom asked, a little doubt creeping into her voice. "You sound kind of down."

"I'm fine," I said, trying to sound a little more alive. "Just kinda tired."

"Okay, then. See you sometime tomorrow. Oh, by the way," she added, and I could hear the wicked grin in her voice, "I gave Becky your love."

I groaned and hung up.

I was warming up a can of beans when Terror came in from about her fiftieth trip to check on Rambo. "Truck turning into the driveway," she announced.

Great, I thought. Company is the last thing we need right now. I looked out the window just in time to see Jana getting out of the passenger door. I had a pretty good idea who the driver would be.

I was right. Chase. Now, on top of everything else, he was going to rag at me for missing my ride. I didn't really blame him. He puts all that work into teaching me. Then, the first rodeo I enter, I don't show and they turn out my stock.

Terror went to the door. Jana came bursting in first. "Layne, what happened? I was so worried about you. I tried to call you all afternoon but I couldn't get you. Why weren't you at the rodeo?"

I sighed and stirred the beans. "It's a long story," I said.

For the first time in my life I was glad when Terror jumped right in and took over the conversation. I felt too lousy about the whole mess to even talk about it.

Finally Terror got to the end of the story. "I tried to tell Layne to go, but he wouldn't leave me and Rambo. So, on account of us, he missed his big ride."

I looked up from setting a couple of plates on the table, amazed. My kid sister was giving me this admiring look. I'd never seen her look at anything but horses like that before. Suddenly I'd become her hero? This was pretty weird. But it didn't change one thing.

Slowly I turned toward Chase. He'd been real quiet, taking the story in. "I'm sorry it turned out this way, Chase," I said, low-voiced. "All the time you spent getting me ready and then my bull gets turned out."

Chase gave me a funny look. "They didn't turn him out," he said.

"What?" I didn't get it. That's what they did when the rider didn't show. Just let the bull out of the chute. No ride. No refunds. No nothing.

Chase rubbed his chin thoughtfully. "Well, I figured when you didn't show up by starting time something had come up. The arena director owed me a favor, so I did some fast talking and got your ride moved into tomorrow's go-round." He paused and gave me a searching look. "If you still want it, that is," he added.

If I still wanted it? Oh, yeah, I wanted it. "All right!" I yelled, managing to knock over the glass of milk I'd just poured. But that didn't matter. Nothing mattered except that I was going to ride.

Chapter Nine

I got to the rodeo grounds early the next day. Too early. I had to kill an hour before I could even find out which bull I'd drawn. I hadn't slept much the night before, wondering about that. Now, the closer I came to finding out, the worse my stomach felt. There were a lot of different bulls out there, but only one picture kept flashing through my mind…

When I finally spotted the rodeo secretary just getting set up beside the announcer's booth, I went charging over there. Then, just in time, I caught myself acting like an over-eager kid and put on the brakes. I strolled the last few steps as if I had all the time in the world. "Hi, Mrs. Henry," I said to the secretary. "I figured maybe I should check on my draw for the bull riding." I pulled out my wallet and handed her the entry fee.

She smiled. "Sure, Layne. I thought your name would turn up in this event sooner or later." She shuffled some papers while I stood there wishing she'd hurry up before this conversation went any further. "Okay, here it is," she said, pulling out a sheet of paper. "I remember now. There was some mix-up and your bull almost got turned out yesterday." She glanced at the paper and gave a low whistle. "Hey, Layne, you picked a good one. Anybody sticks with this guy takes home some money. He was out with a bad foot for a while. I think this is his first time back…"

"Rhino," I almost whispered.

Mrs. Henry gave me a strange look. "You really have been doing your homework on these bulls. It's Rhino, all right. Well, good luck. You'll need it."

"Thanks," I muttered, not too gratefully, and walked away.

A few minutes later I ran into Chase. He was holding a program and looking downright pleased. He winked at me. "Looks like you could be a rich man by the end of the day, huh, kid?"

I swallowed and then forced a smile. "Yeah," I said.

The bull riding wouldn't start for a while, but I got my bag and went behind the chutes to get ready. I got my rope all resined up, and I rubbed in a little glycerin to make it stickier. Then I started doing some warm-ups and stretches to get my muscles loosened up. I wanted to try to burn off some of the nervousness. It seemed to work. I was feeling pretty good by the time they started loading the bulls into the chutes. Then, as I turned to watch, I saw that one big Brahma hump towering above the rest. It was like an ice-cold fist had clenched in my stomach again.

Chase was watching me. "You still think you're ready for him?"

"Rhino? Sure. Why wouldn't I be? Just because I had a little accident that other time doesn't mean anything. Rhino's just another bull to me." Even as I said it I couldn't help wondering if it was Chase I was trying to convince—or myself.

Chase silently chewed his Copenhagen for a minute. "Yeah," he said at last. "That's what he is if that's what you think he is. Come on, let's go get your rope on him."

I nodded and we walked over toward the chutes. All the way Chase's words kept echoing through my mind—*if that's what you think he is*. I knew exactly what Chase meant. Rhino was a tough bull. Everybody knew that. And every bull rider was glad to draw the tough ones. That was where the high-point rides came from. As long as I could think of Rhino as just a tough bull, I'd be okay.

But deep down, that wasn't what I thought. Every time I looked at that big, black, one-horned devil I saw the bull that almost killed me.

I rubbed my hands on my jeans, trying to get rid of the sweat on my palms. My stomach felt real weird.

I concentrated hard on helping Chase get the rigging on. That helped my lunch stay put—temporarily, at least.

There were a lot of other people around the chutes. Some of them talked to me. I think they wished me luck or something. I answered. I don't know what I said but I guess it made sense. Nobody looked at me like I was crazy, anyway.

The bull riding was starting. The first rider out was Jason Thorne. He was good. He'd finished pretty high in the standings last year. He had kind of a small bull named Taco Time. It didn't look too tough, but looks can be deceiving. Taco Time burst out of that chute with a flying leap so high he looked more like a bronc than a bull. He landed with a spine-jarring jolt and started spinning to the right. That was good, I thought. Judges give high marks for a good spinning bull. The bull switched directions, but Jason stayed with him. This was going to be a great ride if he stayed on. Before I could finish that thought the horn sounded and the ride was over. Just eight short seconds, although it could feel like eight of the longest seconds of your life.

I watched as Jason actually chose his moment to let go and pile off to the side, away from both the bull's head and hind feet. He strolled off across the arena, not even looking over his shoulder at the bull. He didn't need to. Taco Time was eagerly making his escape through the gate and out of the arena. I felt a few of the butterflies in my stomach settle down and fold their wings. Maybe Rhino would behave that same way today.

The announcer's voice boomed out. "Eighty-five points for Jason Thorne on Taco Time, ladies and gentlemen, a real fine score for a real fine cowboy," he said, and the crowd went wild. Jason deserved the applause. That was a picture-perfect ride. Never in my wildest dreams was I going to come close to a score like that. That didn't matter. I just wanted to make the ride.

Another rider was coming out of the chute. "Out of chute number three, here comes Mark Greeley on Mr. Clean." The announcer barely had time to say the words before Mr. Clean decided Mark was a piece of dirt and removed him. Mark did a face-plant in the dust right in front of the bull. There was a flash of color and the clown was right there, between the bull and the rider. His job was to distract the bull while the rider got out of there. He was good at it—almost as good as my little sister, I thought, remembering. The bull swerved and charged toward the clown. He dodged easily aside as the pickup men moved in and ran the bull out of the arena.

I began to feel better. The clowns here were good. If I did get in trouble, they'd get Rhino away from me. It was going to be all right. The butterflies were resting comfortably.

There was one more rider before me. I'd never heard his name before so I figured he must be new. Maybe a kid like me just starting out. I watched as, two chutes away, he got down on his bull and got ready. I was only half paying attention to him but something about him bothered me.

Then Chase's voice cut in. "Come on, Layne. Time to get down on your bull."

I eased down on Rhino's back, slid up on my rope and started taking my wraps. I was concentrating hard on what I was doing, but I heard the gate of the other chute slam open. "And out of chute number one, Rusty Barnett on Death Star." I looked up in time to see Death Star go high off the ground and land with a jackhammer jerk and twist.

I winced just thinking about what that must be doing to the guy's back. He was riding him though. He was doing okay.

Come on, I thought. Hang in there. But right then I saw him start to get off-center. He was still hanging on though. But almost his whole body was on the bull's right side now. There was no way he could get it back.

Let go, I thought. You've lost it. Just let go and fall. But he didn't. And suddenly I realized why. He couldn't let go. And then I understood what had been bothering me before. Even at a distance the motions with the rope had been familiar. Suicide wrap.

I didn't want to see this. Not again. I'd seen it six years ago and that was enough for a lifetime. But I couldn't quit staring. He was right off the bull now, bouncing along beside it and being jerked up and down like a puppet. There were two clowns working together now.

One was trying to turn the bull toward himself so the other could move in and jerk the rope loose. It wasn't working though. The bull just kept jumping and twisting. I saw one big front hoof come down on the guy's leg, hard. I could have sworn I heard the bone snap, but maybe I imagined it. I was having trouble keeping things straight right then.

"Oh god, Dad…," I heard myself whisper. I turned my head away and swallowed hard. When I could look again, it was just in time to see the clown finally pull the rope free. The rider dropped to the ground and lay motionless as the bull went on bucking across the arena.

The ambulance was already wheeling into the arena as the announcer tried to calm the crowd. "That's the sort of thing we sure hate to see, ladies and gentlemen. Young fellow got banged up pretty bad. But he's awake and moving down there.

He can hear you. Let's give him a big hand and let him know we're all behind him, folks…"

Yeah, I thought. He's alive. From where I was sitting I could see that. But that didn't say for how long.

The ambulance was leaving now. On with the show. "And coming up in chute number three…"

Chase turned his attention back to me. I could see from his face that he'd been hit hard by what had happened. "Tough luck," he said, shaking his head. Then he took a closer look at me. I guess I must have looked like I was totally freaked. I do know I was shaking all over. "Get off that bull, Layne," Chase ordered. His voice was low but hard as steel. I just stared at him.

I could hear the announcer's voice. It seemed to be coming from a long way off. "…something kind of special today. Layne McQueen, son of Jeff McQueen, who was pretty much a legend around this part of the country. One thing for sure, if Layne's half the bull rider his dad was, he's got a great future ahead of him…"

I took a couple of deep breaths. "Layne!" Chase was yelling in my ear. "You're not ridin' today." I felt his hand dig into my shoulder.

I looked down at the gate man. "Outside!" I yelled.

The gate slammed open and we were in the arena. Rhino had been waiting for a long time. It was time to unwind. He came out of there with a high, bone-jarring jump that just about took the fillings out of my teeth. But it shook all the ghosts out of my head too. All of a sudden, the fear was gone. This was just another bull to ride. All the pieces started falling into place. Chin in. Chest out. Lean back. Pull hard on the rope. Keep your mind in the middle. Just like

Dad had always said. Keep your mind in the middle and that's where the rest of you will be.

Rhino was spinning now. How could eight seconds take so long? Come on, who's timing this thing? It's eight seconds, not eight minutes. Rhino stopped spinning to the left, and a split second later he was spinning to the right. I was getting so dizzy I couldn't see straight. I couldn't be seeing straight because I thought I caught a glimpse of...

And right then two things happened. I lost my concentration and Rhino reversed his spin again. I tried to go with him but, instantly, I knew I was too slow. I was cursing my carelessness as I hit the ground. At that same instant the horn sounded to end the ride. I had come so close.

But I didn't have time to worry about that right now. In my mind I could feel Rhino's hot breath behind me as I ran for the fence. I hauled myself up on the top rail and looked back. I was just in time to see Rhino hit the barrel the clown had rolled toward him and send it flying. Better the barrel than me, I thought, grinning with relief.

Suddenly the grin froze on my face. I hadn't imagined what I thought I'd seen just before I was bucked off. My mom was here. She was running across the arena toward me. I took a deep breath and jumped down to meet her.

We stood there staring at each other. It felt like we were the only two people in the rodeo grounds. I looked at her white, set face and wondered. Was she going to make good her threat and throw me out for riding. Had the ride been worth the risk?

Mom finally broke the heavy silence. "You had to do it, didn't you, Layne?" I couldn't read how she meant it by the tone of her voice. I couldn't even decide if she was asking me or telling me.

I swallowed. "Yeah, Mom," I said softly. "I had to." Please, Mom, understand, I added silently.

She shook her head. "You're crazy," she said. Then her voice turned gentle. "Just as crazy as your dad." She wiped the back of her hand across her eyes, smearing her makeup. "I guess that's why I love you just as much." Suddenly she reached out and gave me a big hug, right there in front of everybody. And it didn't embarrass me. I didn't care if the whole world knew that was my mom.

The next thing I knew, Jana was there. She was hugging me too. "You did great, Layne," she whispered. And then she kissed me. It was really nice. It could have been longer, but, wouldn't you know it, right then Terror came charging up. For a minute I was afraid she might actually hug me too. But then she pulled herself together and punched me on the arm. "Not bad," she said. "For a guy, that is."

I just stood there grinning like a fool. I mean, I fell off the bull and all the women in the world go crazy. I couldn't wait to find out what would happen if I stayed on.

I looked over at the fence where Chase was standing. He just winked.

Marilyn Halvorson is also the author of *Blue Moon*. When she is not caring for cattle on her ranch, Marilyn spends her time writing.

orca soundings

The following is an excerpt from
another exciting Orca Soundings novel,
Blue Moon by Marilyn Halvorson.

978-1-55143-320-2 $9.95 pb

BOBBIE JO DIDN'T SET OUT TO BUY

a limping blue roan mare—she wanted a colt
she could train to barrel race. But the horse is a
fighter, just like Bobbie Jo. Now all she has to do
is train the sour old mare that obviously has a
past. While she nurses the horse back to health,
Bobbie Jo realizes that the horse, now called
Blue Moon, may have more history than she first
thought. With the help of the enigmatic Cole,
she slowly turns the horse into a barrel racer.

Chapter One

"Sold!" the auctioneer yelled. "To the young redhead in the red jacket."

For a second I just sat there stunned. Out of the corner of my eye I could see a curl of hair above the shoulder of my jacket. The hair was red. The jacket was red. There was no getting out of it. I had just bought a horse.

But why had I bought this horse? I watched gloomily as the bony blue roan mare limped out of the sale ring. Her ears were laid back angrily. As the ring man swung the gate closed behind her, she lashed out and kicked it with both back hoofs. Oh, wow! Did I have a winner on my hands! How could I have been so stupid? What was my dad going to say? He lets me go to my first horse sale alone, on a school day even, and I mess up big-time. But sitting here wasn't going to help. Slowly I stood up and made my way down from the stands and toward the sales office.

I was partway through the barn area when a voice stopped me. It was a cool, lazy, laid-back voice. "Skippin' school, Bobbie Jo?"

I swung around and almost bumped into the guy who owned the voice. Cole McCall, the kid from the farm next to ours. Just who I needed to finish wrecking my day. I tossed my hair back. "That's an interesting question. Coming from the all-time champion at that sport," I said coldly.

I turned and kept on walking. Cole just laughed and fell into step beside me. I pretended he wasn't there.

"Where are you goin'?" he asked.

"To pay for my horse, if it's any of your business."

"You just bought a horse?" Cole's voice had taken on a new note of interest.

"That's what I said," I answered, looking straight ahead and walking a little faster. "Now why don't you go find some of your hoodlum friends and leave me alone?"

A look I couldn't quite get flickered across his face. For a second I almost thought there was a real person behind Cole McCall's grin. But then he gave a careless shrug. "Yeah, why not? The guys are better company than you. See ya around, Blue Jeans."

Cole had been calling me that ever since he first came into my grade-ten class at West Valley High School last year. The nickname did fit my initials. It fit my clothes too. But I still didn't want Cole McCall calling me that. I didn't want him calling me anything. Maybe it was because I was afraid he kind of liked me. At least, my friend Julie said he did. But I wasn't about to get involved with a guy like Cole. He had a real attitude. He was always in trouble at school, mainly for skipping, and he didn't even try to come up with a good excuse for it. Besides, I wasn't about to go out with any guy who had longer hair than I did. I tossed my head and marched off to pay for the horse I shouldn't even have bought.

At the office I told the clerk my name and he flipped through some papers.

"Okay, here it is. B.J. Brooks, lot number seventy-nine. All I need is a check for six hundred and ninety dollars." His eyes widened as I dug in my pocket and came out with a fat roll of bills.

"Cash okay?" I asked. I'd emptied my piggy bank, dumped the jar of quarters I'd been saving since I was ten, and taken all the coins to the bank. Then I'd closed out my savings account and taken that in cash too. It looked like a lot of money when I got it all in bills.

The clerk nodded. "Cash is fine. You're just the first person I've seen in a long time who actually has some."

I started counting out the money and thought about how much work I'd done to earn each one of those twenty-dollar bills. The profit from three years of raising 4-H calves, all those summers of cutting the neighbors' lawns. And I'd gathered up every cent and brought it here to buy this horse.

No, that wasn't true. I didn't bring it here to buy this horse. I came to buy a colt. A yearling at the oldest. A good, young quarter horse that I could train myself and make into a champion barrel horse. Buying a colt would mean it would be three or four years before I could actually race him. I hated waiting that long, but I didn't have a choice. If you watched your chance, you could get a good colt for the money I had. A trained barrel horse, ready to go, would cost a few thousand.

So how had I set out to buy a colt with a future and wound up with a sour, beat-up old mare that obviously had a past? I'd asked myself that question a lot of times in the last few minutes, but I still wasn't sure of the answer.

I should have realized from the start that the blue roan mare was a meat horse. If I hadn't known by the way she looked, I should have known by who was bidding on her. There were a couple of crafty old guys who always hung around the sales, picking up the horses that had hit the end of the trail. They bought for the meat packers and they were always on the lookout for a chance to buy cheap. Much as I hated the thought of any horse ending up that way, I knew it was a fact of life. I guess it was better than the horses being left to starve. Better than getting so old and crippled they got down and couldn't get up.

So why couldn't I have just left things alone and let nature take its course? Why did I have to go and buy this mare? It might have been her color that did it. When I was a little kid I had a picture book called *Lady, the Little Blue Mare*. It was about a blue roan horse, and I read it until the cover fell off. Ever since, I'd wanted a horse that color more than anything else in the world. But blue roans are about as common as honest politicians. I guess I went a little crazy when I came across a blue roan I could actually own. Or maybe the real reason I bought her was because she was a rebel. I liked the way she held her head up. The way she fought back when she was pushed around.

While one half of my mind was thinking about that, the other half was counting out the money. "Six hundred, six hundred and twenty, six hundred and forty, six hundred and sixty, six hundred and eighty," I counted out loud. Suddenly I stopped. That was my last twenty I'd just tossed on the pile. I dug in my pocket for the other twenty I knew was there. Nothing but a well-worn Kleenex. I checked the other pocket. Empty as my kid sister's head. I checked the pockets of my jean jacket. Lint and two gum wrappers.

The clerk cleared his throat. "Another ten dollars, miss."

"I know, I know," I muttered, shooting him a dirty look. "Don't get your shirt in a knot. It's here somewhere." I made another panic-stricken tour of my pockets. That twenty dollars was not here anywhere. I could hear the people in the lineup behind me shuffling their feet.

"Miss," the clerk said firmly, "either you've got the money or you haven't. If you're short on cash, why don't you write a check for the last ten?"

"Because I don't have any money left in the bank," I muttered. "But I did have the cash. I know I did."

"Well," the clerk said wearily, "you don't now. Step aside and let these other people go ahead. I'll give you half an hour to come up with the cash or we'll have to resell the horse."

Resell the horse? Let him resell the horse and I'd be off the hook. I'd have my $690.00 and I wouldn't be stuck with that sorry excuse for an animal. I should have jumped right up and kissed that old clerk on his tobacco-stained mustache. But, oh no, not me. Right then and there I bristled up like a cornered cat and glared at him. "You will not resell that horse. I bought her fair and square and I'll get you your lousy ten bucks. You can count on it!"

Titles in the Series

orca soundings

Back
Norah McClintock

Bang
Norah McClintock

Battle of the Bands
K.L. Denman

Big Guy
Robin Stevenson

Blue Moon
Marilyn Halvorson

Breathless
Pam Withers

Bull Rider
Marilyn Halvorson

Bull's Eye
Sarah N. Harvey

Charmed
Carrie Mac

Chill
Colin Frizzell

Comeback
Vicki Grant

Crush
Carrie Mac

The Darwin Expedition
Diane Tullson

Dead-End Job
Vicki Grant

Death Wind
William Bell

Down
Norah McClintock

Exit Point
Laura Langston

Exposure
Patricia Murdoch

Fastback Beach
Shirlee Smith Matheson

First Time
Meg Tilly

Grind
Eric Walters

Hannah's Touch
Laura Langston

The Hemingway Tradition
Kristin Butcher

Hit Squad
James Heneghan

Home Invasion
Monique Polak

House Party
Eric Walters

I.D.
Vicki Grant

Impact
James C. Dekker

In the Woods
Robin Stevenson

Jacked
Carrie Mac

Juice
Eric Walters

Kicked Out
Beth Goobie

Learning to Fly
Paul Yee

Lockdown
Diane Tullson

Middle Row
Sylvia Olsen

My Time as Caz Hazard
Tanya Lloyd Kyi

No More Pranks
Monique Polak

No Problem
Dayle Campbell Gaetz

One More Step
Sheree Fitch

Overdrive
Eric Walters

Pain & Wastings
Carrie Mac

Picture This
Norah McClintock

Plastic
Sarah N. Harvey

Reaction
Lesley Choyce

Refuge Cove
Lesley Choyce

Responsible
Darlene Ryan

Riley Park
Diane Tullson

Rock Star
Adrian Chamberlain

Running the Risk
Lesley Choyce

Saving Grace
Darlene Ryan

Scum
James C. Dekker

Snitch
Norah McClintock

Something Girl
Beth Goobie

Spiral
K.L. Denman

Sticks and Stones
Beth Goobie

Stuffed
Eric Walters

Tell
Norah McClintock

Thunderbowl
Lesley Choyce

Tough Trails
Irene Morck

The Trouble with Liberty
Kristin Butcher

Truth
Tanya Lloyd Kyi

Wave Warrior
Lesley Choyce

Who Owns Kelly Paddik?
Beth Goobie

Yellow Line
Sylvia Olsen

Zee's Way
Kristin Butcher